Epicurus

341 BC–270 BC

Epicurus
Being Happy

Translated by George K. Strodach

PENGUIN BOOKS — GREAT IDEAS

PENGUIN BOOKS

UK | USA | Canada | Ireland | Australia
India | New Zealand | South Africa

Penguin Books is part of the Penguin Random House group
of companies whose addresses can be found at
global.penguinrandomhouse.com.

Penguin
Random House
UK

Essays originally published in *The Art of Happiness*,
Penguin Classics 2013
This selection published in Penguin Books 2020
 004

Translation copyright © John K. Strodach, 2013

Set in 11.2/13.75 pt Dante MT Std
Typeset by Jouve (UK), Milton Keynes
Printed and bound in Great Britain by Clays Ltd, Elcograf S.p.A.

A CIP catalogue record for this book
is available from the British Library

ISBN: 978-0-241-47326-9

www.greenpenguin.co.uk

MIX
Paper from
responsible sources
FSC® C018179

Penguin Random House is committed to a
sustainable future for our business, our readers
and our planet. This book is made from Forest
Stewardship Council® certified paper.

Contents

Letter to Menoeceus

No one should postpone the study of philosophy when he is young, nor should he weary of it when he becomes mature, because the search for mental health is never untimely or out of season. To say that the time to study philosophy has not yet arrived or that it is past is like saying that the time for happiness is not yet at hand or is no longer present. Thus both the young and the mature should pursue philosophy, the latter in order to be rejuvenated as they age by the blessings that accrue from pleasurable past experience, and the youthful in order to become mature immediately through having no fear of the future. Hence we should make a practice of the things that make for happiness, for assuredly when we have this we have everything, and we do everything we can to get it when we don't have it.

THE PRECONDITIONS OF HAPPINESS

I. You should do and practice all the things I constantly recommended to you, with the knowledge that they are the fundamentals of the good life. (1) First of all, you should think of deity as imperishable and blessed being (as delineated in the universal conception of it common to all men), and you should not attribute to it anything foreign to its immortality or inconsistent with its blessedness. On the contrary, you should hold every doctrine that is capable of safeguarding its blessedness in common with its imperishability. The gods do indeed exist, since our knowledge of them is a matter of clear and distinct perception; but they are not like what the masses suppose them to be, because most people do not maintain the pure conception of the gods. The irreligious man is not the person who destroys the gods of the masses but the person who imposes the ideas of the masses on the gods. The opinions held by most people about the gods are not true conceptions of them but fallacious notions, according to which awful penalties are meted out to the evil and the greatest of blessings to the good. The masses, by assimilating the gods in every respect to their own moral qualities, accept deities similar to themselves and regard anything not of this sort as alien.

(2) Second, you should accustom yourself to believing that death means nothing to us, since every good and every evil lies in sensation; but death is the privation of sensation. Hence a correct comprehension of the fact that death means nothing to us makes the mortal aspect of life pleasurable, not by conferring on us a boundless period of time but by removing the yearning for deathlessness. There is nothing fearful in living for the person who has really laid hold of the fact that there is nothing fearful in not living. So it is silly for a person to say that he dreads death – not because it will be painful when it

arrives but because it pains him now as a future certainty; for that which makes no trouble for us when it arrives is a meaningless pain when we await it. This, the most horrifying of evils, means nothing to us, then, because so long as we are existent death is not present and whenever it is present we are nonexistent. Thus it is of no concern either to the living or to those who have completed their lives. For the former it is nonexistent, and the latter are themselves nonexistent.

Most people, however, recoil from death as though it were the greatest of evils; at other times they welcome it as the end-all of life's ills. The sophisticated person, on the other hand, neither begs off from living nor dreads not living. Life is not a stumbling block to him, nor does he regard not being alive as any sort of evil. As in the case of food he prefers the most savory dish to merely the larger portion, so in the case of time he garners to himself the most agreeable moments rather than the longest span.

Anyone who urges the youth to lead a good life but counsels the older man to end his life in good style is silly, not merely because of the welcome character of life but because of the fact that living well and dying well are one and the same discipline. Much worse off, however, is the person who says it were well not to have been born 'but once born to pass Hades' portals as swiftly as may be.' Now if he says such a thing from inner persuasion why does he not withdraw from life? Everything is in readiness for him once he has firmly resolved on this course. But if he speaks facetiously he is a trifler standing in the midst of men who do not welcome him.

It should be borne in mind, then, that the time to come is neither ours nor altogether not ours. In this way we shall neither expect the future outright as something destined to be nor despair of it as something absolutely not destined to be.

THE GOOD LIFE

II. It should be recognized that within the category of desire certain desires are natural, certain others unnecessary and trivial; that in the case of the natural desires certain ones are necessary, certain others merely natural; and that in the case of necessary desires certain ones are necessary for happiness, others to promote freedom from bodily discomfort, others for the maintenance of life itself. A steady view of these matters shows us how to refer all moral choice and aversion to bodily health and imperturbability of mind, these being the twin goals of happy living. It is on this account that we do everything we do – to achieve freedom from pain and freedom from fear. When once we come by this, the tumult in the soul is calmed and the human being does not have to go about looking for something that is lacking or to search for something additional with which to supplement the welfare of soul and body. Accordingly we have need of pleasure only when we feel pain because of the absence of pleasure, but whenever we do not feel pain we no longer stand in need of pleasure. And so we speak of pleasure as the starting point and the goal of the happy life because we realize that it is our primary native good, because every act of choice and aversion originates with it, and because we come back to it when we judge every good by using the pleasure feeling as our criterion.

Because of the very fact that pleasure is our primary and congenital good we do not select every pleasure; there are times when we forgo certain pleasures, particularly when they are followed by too much unpleasantness. Furthermore, we regard certain states of pain as preferable to pleasures, particularly when greater satisfaction results from our having submitted to discomforts for a long period of time. Thus every pleasure is a good by reason of its having a nature akin to our own, but not every pleasure is desirable. In like manner every state of pain is an evil, but not all pains are uniformly to be rejected. At any rate, it is our duty to judge all such cases by measuring pleasures against pains, with a view to their respective assets and liabilities, inasmuch as we do experience the good as being bad at times and, contrariwise, the bad as being good.

In addition, we consider limitation of the appetites a major good, and we recommend this practice not for the purpose of enjoying just a few things and no more but rather for the purpose of enjoying those few in case we do not have much. We are firmly convinced that those who need expensive fare least are the ones who relish it most keenly and that a natural way of life is easily procured, while trivialities are hard to come by. Plain foods afford pleasure equivalent to that of a sumptuous diet, provided that the pains of penury are wholly eliminated. Barley bread and water yield the peak of pleasure whenever a person who needs them sets them in front of himself. Hence becoming habituated to a simple rather than a lavish way of life provides us with the full complement of health; it makes a person ready for the necessary business of life; it puts us in a position of advantage when we happen upon sumptuous fare at intervals and prepares us to be fearless in facing fortune.

Thus when I say that pleasure is the goal of living I do not mean the pleasures of libertines or the pleasures inherent in positive enjoyment, as is supposed by certain persons who are ignorant of our doctrine or who are not in agreement with it or who interpret it perversely. I mean, on the contrary, the pleasure that consists in freedom from bodily pain and mental agitation. The pleasant life is not the product of one drinking party after another or of sexual intercourse with women and boys or of the sea food and other delicacies afforded by a luxurious table. On the contrary, it is the result of sober thinking – namely, investigation of the reasons for every act of choice and aversion and elimination of those false ideas about the gods and death which are the chief source of mental disturbances.

The starting point of this whole scheme and the most important of its values is good judgment, which consequently is more highly esteemed even than philosophy. All the other virtues stem from sound judgment, which shows us that it is impossible to live the pleasant Epicurean life without also living sensibly, nobly, and justly and, vice versa, that it is impossible to live sensibly, nobly, and justly without living pleasantly. The traditional virtues grow up together with the pleasant life; they are indivisible. Can you think of anyone more moral than the person who has devout beliefs about the gods, who is consistently without fears about death, and who has pondered man's natural end? Or who realizes that the goal of the good life is easily gained and achieved and that the term of evil is brief, both in extent of time and duration of pain? Or the man who laughs at the 'decrees of Fate,' a deity whom some people have set up as sovereign of all?

The good Epicurean believes that certain events occur deterministically, that others are chance events, and that still others are in our own hands. He sees also that necessity cannot be held morally responsible and that chance is an unpredictable thing, but that what is in our own hands, since it has no master, is naturally associated with blameworthiness and the opposite. (Actually it would be better to subscribe to the popular mythology than to become a slave by accepting the determinism of the natural philosophers, because popular religion underwrites the hope of supplicating the gods by offerings but determinism contains an element of necessity, which is inexorable.) As for chance, the Epicurean does not assume that it is a deity (as in popular belief) because a god does nothing irregular; nor does he regard it as an unpredictable cause of all events. It is

his belief that good and evil are not the chance contribu-
tions of a deity, donated to mankind for the happy life,
but rather that the initial circumstances for great good
and evil are sometimes provided by chance. He thinks
it preferable to have bad luck rationally than good luck
irrationally. In other words, in human action it is better
for a rational choice to be unsuccessful than for an
irrational choice to succeed through the agency of
chance.

Think about these and related matters day and night,
by yourself and in company with someone like yourself.
If you do, you will never experience anxiety, waking or
sleeping, but you will live like a god among men. For a
human being who lives in the midst of immortal blessings is in no way like mortal man!

Leading Doctrines

1–5: Five Fundamental Teachings Bearing on the Good Life.

1. The blessed and indestructible being of the divine has no concerns of its own, nor does it make trouble for others. It is not affected by feelings of anger or benevolence, because these are found where there is lack of strength.

2. Death means nothing to us, because that which has been broken down into atoms has no sensation and that which has no sensation is no concern of ours.

3. The quantitative limit of pleasure is the elimination of all feelings of pain. Wherever the pleasurable state exists, there is neither bodily pain nor mental pain nor both together, so long as the state continues.

4. Bodily pain does not last continuously. The peak is present for a very brief period, and pains that barely exceed the state of bodily pleasure do not continue for many days. On the other hand, protracted illnesses show a balance of bodily pleasure over pain.

5. It is impossible to live the pleasant life without also living sensibly, nobly, and justly, and conversely it is impossible to live sensibly, nobly, and justly without living pleasantly. A person who does not have a pleasant life is not living sensibly, nobly, and justly, and conversely the person who does not have these virtues cannot live pleasantly.

6–7: Personal Security and the Good Life.

6. Any means by which it is possible to procure freedom from fearing other men is a natural good.

7. Some men have desired to gain reputation and to be well regarded, thinking in this way to gain protection from other people. If the lives of such men are secure, they have acquired a natural blessing; but if they are not, they do not possess what they originally reached for by natural instinct.

8–9: How to Choose Pleasures.

8. No pleasure is bad in itself. But the things that make for pleasure in certain cases entail disturbances many times greater than the pleasures themselves.

9. If all pleasures could be compressed in time and intensity, and were characteristic of the whole man or his more important aspects, the various pleasures would not differ from each other.

10–13: The Good Life Is Dependent on Science.

10. If the things that produce the debauchee's pleasures dissolved the mind's fears regarding the heavenly bodies, death, and pain and also told us how to limit our desires, we would never have any reason to find fault with such people, because they would be glutting themselves with every sort of pleasure and never suffer physical or mental pain, which is the real evil.

11. We would have no need for natural science unless we were worried by apprehensiveness regarding the heavenly bodies, by anxiety about the meaning of death, and also by our failure to understand the limitations of pain and desire.

12. It is impossible to get rid of our anxieties about essentials if we do not understand the nature of the universe and are apprehensive about some of the theological accounts. Hence it is impossible to enjoy our pleasures unadulterated without natural science.

13. There is no advantage in gaining security with regard to other people if phenomena occurring above and beneath the earth – in a word, everything in the infinite universe – are objects of anxiety.

14: Withdrawal into Obscurity Is the Best Form of Security.

14. The simplest means of procuring protection from other men (which is gained to a certain extent by deterrent force) is the security of quiet solitude and withdrawal from the mass of people.

15: Wealth, Natural and Unnatural.

15. Nature's wealth is restricted and easily won, while that of empty convention runs on to infinity.

16: Luck vs. Reason in the Good Life.

16. Bad luck strikes the sophisticated man in a few cases, but reason has directed the big, essential things, and for the duration of life it is and will be the guide.

17: Justice and Mental Health.

17. The just man is the least disturbed by passion, the unjust man the most highly disturbed.

18–21: The Limits of True Pleasure.

18. Bodily pleasure is not enlarged once the pains brought on by need have been done away with; it is only diversified. And the limit of mental pleasure is established by rational reflection on pleasures themselves and those kindred emotions that once instilled extreme fear in human minds.

19. Infinite time contains no greater pleasure than does finite time, if one determines the limits of pleasure rationally.

20. The body takes the limits of pleasure to be infinite, and infinite time would provide such pleasure. But the mind has provided us with the complete life by a rational examination of the body's goal and limitations and by dispelling our fears about a life after death; and so we no longer need unlimited time. On the other hand, it does not avoid pleasure,

nor, when conditions occasion our departure from life, does it come to the end in a manner that would suggest that it had fallen short in any way of the best possible existence.

21. One who understands the limits of the good life knows that what eliminates the pains brought on by need and what makes the whole of life perfect is easily obtained, so that there is no need for enterprises that entail the struggle for success.

22–25: Empirical Considerations.

22. It is necessary to take into account both the actual goal of life and the whole body of clear and distinct percepts to which we refer our judgments. If we fail to do this, everything will be in disorder and confusion.

23. If you reject all sensations, you will not have any point of reference by which to judge even the ones you claim are false.

24. If you summarily rule out any single sensation and do not make a distinction between the element of belief that is superimposed on a percept that awaits verification and what is actually present in sensation or in the feelings or some percept of the mind itself, you will cast doubt on all other sensations by your unfounded interpretation and consequently abandon all the criteria of truth. On the other hand, in cases of interpreted data, if you accept as true those that need verification as well as those that do not, you will still be in error, since the whole question at issue in every

judgment of what is true or not true will be left intact.

25. If at any time you fail to refer each of your acts to nature's standard, and turn off instead in some other direction when making a choice to avoid or pursue, your actions will not be consistent with your creed.

26, 29, 30: Classification of Human Desires.

29. Some desires are (1) natural and necessary, others (2) natural but not necessary, still others (3) neither natural nor necessary but generated by senseless whims.

26. All desires that do not lead to physical pain if not satisfied are unnecessary, and involve cravings that are easily resolved when they appear to entail harm or when the object of desire is hard to get.

30. If interest is intense in the case of those natural desires that do not lead to physical pain when they are not satisfied, then such desires are generated by idle fancy, and it is not because of their own nature that they are not dissipated but because of the person's own senseless whims.

27–28: Friendship.

27. Of all the things that wisdom provides for the happiness of the whole man, by far the most important is the acquisition of friendship.

28. It is the same judgment that has made us feel confident that nothing fearful is of long duration or everlasting, and that has seen personal security

during our limited span of life most nearly perfected by friendship.

31–38: Justice and Injustice.

31. The justice that seeks nature's goal is a utilitarian pledge of men not to harm each other or be harmed.

32. Nothing is either just or unjust in the eyes of those animals that have been unable to make agreements not to harm each other or be harmed. The same is true of those peoples who are unable or unwilling to make covenants not to harm or be harmed.

33. Justice was never an entity in itself. It is a kind of agreement not to harm or be harmed, made when men associate with each other at any time and in communities of any size whatsoever.

34. Injustice is not an evil in itself. Its evil lies in the anxious fear that you will not elude those who have authority to punish such misdeeds.

35. It is impossible for a person who underhandedly breaks the agreement not to harm or be harmed to feel sure that he will escape punishment, even though he manages to do so time after time; for up to the very end of his life he cannot be sure that he will actually escape.

36. In its general meaning, justice is the same for all because of its utility in the relations of men to each other, but in its specific application to countries and various other circumstances it does not follow that the same thing is just for all.

37. In the case of actions that are legally regarded as just, those that are of tested utility in meeting the needs of human society have the hallmark of justice, whether they turn out to be equally just in all cases or not. On the other hand, if somebody lays down a law and it does not prove to be of advantage in human relations, then such a law no longer has the true character of justice. And even if the element of utility should undergo a change after harmonizing for a time with the conception of justice, the law was still just during that period, in the judgment of those who are not confused by meaningless words but who look at the actualities.

38. In cases where the surrounding conditions are not new and where laws regarded as just have been shown to be inconsistent with the conception of justice in their actual workings, such laws are unjust. Again, in cases where the circumstances are new and where the same laws, once deemed to be just, are no longer serviceable, the laws in this case were just as long as they were useful to the community of citizens, but later when they were no longer useful they became unjust.

39–40: The Sectarian Spirit and Life.

39. The person who is the most successful in controlling the disturbing elements that come from the outside world has assimilated to himself what he could, and what he could not assimilate he has at least not alienated. Where he could not do even this, he has

dissociated himself or eliminated all that it was
expedient to treat in this way.

40. All who have the capacity to gain security,
especially from those who live around them, live a
most agreeable life together, since they have the
firm assurance of friendship; and after enjoying their
comradeship to the full they do not bewail the early
demise of a departed friend as if it were a pitiable
thing.

The Vatican Collection of Aphorisms

4. All pain is readily discounted. Intense pain has a short life, and longer lasting bodily pain is weak.

9. Necessity is bad, but there is no necessity to live under necessity.

11. For most people leisure is stupor, and activity frenzy.

14. We are born once. We cannot be born a second time, and throughout eternity we shall of necessity no longer exist. You have no power over the morrow, and yet you put off your pleasure. Life is ruined by procrastination, and every one of us dies deep in his affairs.

18. If you subtract seeing, social contact, and sexual intercourse, the erotic passion dissolves.

23. Every friendship is desirable for itself, but it has its origin in personal advantage.

24. Dreams have neither divine character nor prophetic power but are generated by the influx of atomic images.

25. Poverty, when measured by the goals that nature has set, is great wealth, whereas unlimited wealth is great poverty.

29. When discoursing on nature I personally should prefer to speak oracularly, even though no one were

likely to listen, and candidly utter truths that are beneficial to all men, rather than acquiesce in conventional opinion and reap a fat harvest of popular plaudits.

31. It is possible to get protection against other things, but when it comes to death, all of us human beings live in a city without walls.

34. It is not so much friends' services that we find serviceable as the assurance of their services.

37. As regards evil, human nature is feeble – not as regards good; for we are protected by pleasure but destroyed by pain.

38. The person who has a number of good reasons for making his exit from life is puny indeed.

40. The person who says that everything happens necessarily cannot criticize the person who says that things do not happen necessarily; for he has to admit that this too is a necessary happening!

41. We must laugh and philosophize and manage our households and look after our other affairs all at the same time, and never stop proclaiming the words of the true philosophy.

44. The wise man, after adjusting himself to the bare necessities of life, understands better how to share than to take – so large is the fund of self-sufficiency that he has discovered.

45. The study of nature does not cause men to give out big words and boasts or to show off those accomplishments that the public fights over; it makes them disdainful and independent, puffed up over

their own good qualities rather than the worth of their possessions.

48. We must try to make the latter part of the journey better than the first, so long as we are en route; and when we reach the end, we must keep an even keel and remain cheerful.

51. I learn from your letter that carnal disturbances make you excessively inclined to sexual intercourse. Well, so long as you do not break any laws or disturb well-established conventions or annoy any of your neighbors or wear down your body or use up your funds, you may carry out your own plans as you like. However, it is impossible not to be affected by at least one of these things. Sex never benefited any man, and it's a marvel if it hasn't injured him!

52. Friendship dances round the world, summoning every one of us to awaken to the gospel of the happy life.

53. We should envy no man. The good are undeserving of envy; as for the bad, the more successful they are, the more they mutilate themselves.

58. We must get out of the prison house of routine duties and politics.

59. It is not the belly that cannot be satisfied, as people believe, but the false belief about the belly's having unlimited capacity.

60. Every man departs this life as though he had just been born.

64. Approval on the part of others must come voluntarily; it is our business to get on with our own self-therapy.

65. It is senseless to ask the gods for what a man is able to provide for himself.

66. Let us show our sympathy for our departed friends not by mourning them but by taking thought.

67. A free man cannot acquire many possessions, because this is no easy feat without becoming a hireling of mobs or dynasts. And yet he has a constant abundance of everything, and if he should chance to gain many possessions, he could easily portion them out so as to win his neighbors' good will.

68. Nothing is sufficient for the person who finds sufficiency too little.

71. We must put the following question to each of our desires: What will happen to me if the object of my desire is achieved? What will happen if it is not?

77. The most important consequence of self-sufficiency is freedom.

79. The impassive soul disturbs neither itself nor others.

81. Spiritual disorder cannot be resolved – or joy worthy of the name produced – by wealth however great, by popular acclaim and respect, or by anything that causes unrestrained desire.

Letter to Herodotus

I. INTRODUCTION

I have already prepared a compendium of my entire philosophy, Herodotus, for the benefit of those who are unable to study methodically all the many volumes on nature that I have written or to examine closely the major works I have composed, in order that they may thereby get an adequate grasp of the most important doctrines at least and may be able to get help from time to time with the leading ideas, to the extent that they concern themselves with physical theory. Also, those who are sufficiently advanced in their survey of the complete works need to refresh their memories with a sketch of the fundamentals of the entire philosophy, because one frequently needs a comprehensive grasp of things and not so much a knowledge of particulars. One must return to the fundamentals and constantly keep in mind just enough to provide an authoritative grasp of the Epicurean system, and then the scientific knowledge of particulars will all be forthcoming, once the comprehensive outlines are firmly grasped and remembered. With the accomplished Epicurean also, the hallmark of full scientific knowledge is the ability to exercise rapid comprehension (both sensory and intellectual), and this can come about only when everything is reduced to fundamental principles and formulas. For a condensation of the entire cycle of my works is impossible unless one can mentally compass in abbreviated formulas all that could be methodically expounded in the form of particulars. Since a procedure of this sort is serviceable to all who are at home in natural philosophy and since I recommend the constant pursuit of natural philosophy and find serenity myself primarily in a life of this sort, I have accordingly written for you a kind of primer and compendium of the whole body of my doctrines.

II. METHODOLOGY

First of all, then, Herodotus, we must grasp the meanings associated with the word sounds in order that, by referring to these, we may be in a position to form judgments about matters of belief or about problems needing research or unresolved questions, and in order to avoid leaving matters in a state of confusion by expounding terms *ad infinitum* or by using meaningless verbiage. We must therefore look to the primary meaning in the case of each word and not require argument if we are to have a point of reference for our research problems, our unresolved questions, or matters of belief. Furthermore, we must keep all our judgments in line with our sensations (specifically our immediate perceptions, either of the mind or of any particular sense organ) and also in line with our actual feelings of pleasure and pain, in order to have the means with which to interpret a sense datum awaiting verification or a problem involving imperceptibles.

III. FIRST PRINCIPLES AND POSTULATES

1. Having made these distinctions, we must now take a synoptic view of imperceptibles: to begin with, the principle that nothing is generated from the nonexistent. This is so because otherwise anything could be generated from anything and not require seminal particles. Second, if an object that passes from our view were completely annihilated, everything in the world would have perished, since that into which things were dissipated would be the nonexistent. Third, the totality of things was always just as it is at present and will always remain the same because there is nothing into which it can change, inasmuch as there is nothing outside the totality that could intrude and effect change.

2. Furthermore, the totality consists of bodies and space. The fact of sensation itself universally attests that there are bodies, and it is by reference to sensation that we must rationally infer the existence of imperceptible bodies, as I remarked previously. If what we call 'the void' or 'space' or 'impalpable being' were nonexistent, bodies would not have anywhere to exist, nor would they have a medium through which to move, as they manifestly do. In addition to these two entities it is

impossible to think of anything else (by way of either concepts or analogues of concepts) as being a complete and independent entity and not, rather, a property or accident of body and space. As regards bodies, further-more, some are compounds; others are the components of which the compounds are made. These components are irreducible and immutable atoms – assuming that things are not destined to be completely annihilated but that something perdurable is left over at the time of the decomposition of the compounds – particles completely solid in nature and incapable of decomposition in any manner whatsoever. Thus the primal entities are neces-sarily indivisible corporeal atoms.

3. Furthermore, the totality of things is unlimited, because anything limited has an end point and this end point is seen against something else. But the totality, having no end point, has no limit and, having no limit, it must be infinite and without boundaries. In addition, the totality is infinite both in the quantity of atomic bodies and in spatial magnitude, because (1) if space were infinite but the atomic bodies finite in number, the atoms would not remain in any position but would be borne about and dispersed throughout infinite space, not having supporting bodies to stabilize them in their recoil from other atoms; and (2) if space were finite, the infinite number of atoms could not find positions anywhere.

4. In addition, the compact and irreducible atomic bodies out of which compounds are generated and into which they are resolved have an indeterminate number

of different shapes, because it is impossible for so many different perceptible objects to be generated from the same shapes on the assumption that these are limited in number. Thus for each atomic configuration the number of similar atoms is plainly infinite; the various configurations, however, are plainly not infinite but simply indeterminate in number.

5. The atoms, furthermore, are in constant motion through endless time. [Some move perpendicularly; others deviate from the perpendicular; still others move by internal vibration within compounds. Of the latter] some are separated by a considerable distance from each other, while others maintain an oscillating motion whenever they find themselves turned aside by intertwining with others or enveloped by an outer casing of atoms. The reason for this internal vibration is that the nature of the empty space that separates the individual atoms produces this effect, since it is unable to provide any support, and also the solidity characteristic of the atoms causes them to rebound after collision to the extent that intertwining permits re-establishment of motion after collision. These vibrations have no starting point, the atoms themselves and empty space being the causes. Now, if all these points are borne in mind, this brief account suggests an outline adequate for comprehending the physical nature of things.

6. In addition, there are infinite worlds – worlds like and unlike our own – because the atoms, being infinite in number, as was just now shown, are in motion extremely far out in space; and atoms of the sort from

which a single world could be generated, or by which
such a single world could be constructed, have not been
used up on one world or on a finite number of worlds,
nor have they been used up on all worlds such as ours
or on all worlds different from ours. So nothing stands
in the way of there being an infinity of worlds.

IV. SENSE PERCEPTION

1. Sight. In addition, there are atomic images similar in
outline to solid external objects but differing greatly
from these in their thinness or non-solidity. It is not
impossible that such atomic discharges should be generated in the environment of objects, nor that suitable
circumstances for the production of these hollow, thin
films should exist, nor that these emanations should
maintain the successive positions and structure that the
particles had in the solid external bodies. We term these
images *eidola*.

Also, nothing in our sensory experience witnesses
against the fact that the *eidola* have an extraordinary
thinness of composition, from which we may also infer
that they have extraordinary speeds, since all their
atoms have uniform velocities in addition to the fact
that their outflow meets with little or no resistance,
whereas structures composed of many or innumerable
atoms do immediately encounter resistance. In addition
to this, there is the fact that the generating of *eidola*
occurs as fast as a man can think, because the outflow
from the surface of objects is continuous (but this does

not become evident in loss of size because the atoms are replenished) and it maintains for a considerable period the position and structure of the atoms of the external object, even though at times it is thrown into disorder. Then, too, composite *eidola* are rapidly formed in the surrounding atmosphere because of the fact that it is unnecessary for the filling-up process to take place in depth; and there are various other ways in which composite images of this sort are generated. None of these points, indeed, is contradicted by our sensory experiences if one will only inspect the manner in which sensation conveys to us clear and distinct images of external objects and their qualities.

One must also assume that when *eidola* impinge on us from external objects we both see and think about their forms; for such objects could not imprint their natural colors and shapes by means of an atmospheric impression formed midway between them and us, nor again by ocular rays or any conceivable emanation originating with us and moving out to the object. These theories are less credible than my own hypothesis that certain atomic films having the same colors and shapes as their objects impinge on us, entering either the eye or the mind, depending on the relative sizes of their atoms; that these films have a rapid course of movement and for this reason present the phenomenon of a unitary and continuously existent object; and that they preserve the qualitative changes of the underlying physical object in their uniform impact on us from that source, which results from the atomic pulsations deep within the physical object.

Also, any perception of shape or qualities that we receive by atomic impingement on the mind or sense organs represents the true shape or quality of the physical object and is generated by the unbroken series of films or its residues, whereas falsity and error always consist of the element of belief superimposed on a percept which awaits verification or noncontradiction and which is then not verified or is contradicted. Thus the correspondence between the perceptions that we take as representations (whether generated in our sleep or in our waking acts of attention, either mental or sensory) and what we call real existent objects could never arise unless certain entities of this sort were making their impact on us. On the other hand, error would not occur unless we were experiencing another kind of internal motion also, one connected with perceptualization but distinct from it. By virtue of this, an untrue judgment occurs whenever this process does not undergo verification or is disconfirmed and a true judgment whenever it is verified or not disconfirmed. It is, therefore, absolutely necessary to maintain this principle in order to prevent the standards of judgment that involve clear and distinct perceptions from being abridged and likewise to prevent error from becoming entrenched and confounding everything.

2. Hearing. Hearing also occurs when a flow of atoms moves off from anything that talks or makes a sound or noise or produces an acoustic reaction in any way whatsoever. This outflow is broken up into atomic masses having similar parts, and these masses simultaneously

preserve a corresponding structure as well as a specific identity that extends back to the point of origin and in most cases causes perception in the person or else simply renders the external object obvious. Indeed, aural perception would not occur unless a corresponding atomic structure were conveyed from the point of origin to the hearer. Accordingly one should not imagine that the atmosphere as such is given a shape by the words we utter or by kindred sounds (for it would require a great deal for it to be affected in this way), but rather that the percussion that occurs internally whenever we utter sounds immediately causes the ejection of certain atomic masses (these effecting an outflow having the nature of breath), which produce in us an auditory reaction.

3. Smell. In the case of smell, furthermore, as in the case of hearing, we must again suppose that nothing would ever produce this reaction except certain atomic masses that move off from the object and are suited to activating the sense organ – some of them in an irregular manner foreign to its make-up, others in an orderly manner congenial to it.

V. ATOMS AND THEIR CHARACTERISTICS

1. Properties of Atoms. In addition, we should note that atoms do not present any of the characteristics of phenomena except shape, weight, and size and everything that is necessarily associated with shape. All phenomenal qualities change, but the atoms do not

change in any way because something has to remain firm and irreducible when compounds are broken up, something that will bring about change – not change into nonbeing or from nonbeing but changes produced by the transposition of certain atoms or by the addition or subtraction of others. Hence it is necessary that these transposed atoms be indestructible and not have the nature of changing phenomena, but have particles and structures peculiar to themselves; for at least this much must remain immutable. Even in the case of objects all around us that undergo change of form through attrition we observe that shape persists, whereas qualities do not persist in the changing body in the same way as shape but disappear entirely. Thus it is the residual atoms that are sufficient to bring about differences in compounds, inasmuch as some bodies at any rate must be residual and not subject to annihilation.

In order not to run the risk of being contradicted by phenomena, we should not assume that all sizes of atom are to be found but only that certain variations in size exist, because on this assumption our affective and sensory experience will be better accounted for. In any case the existence of all sizes of atoms is of no use in accounting for qualitative differences, and furthermore certain sizes would have to come within our sensory range and become visible; but this we never observe, nor is it possible to conceive how an atom could become visible.

2. Parts of the Atom. Furthermore, it should not be assumed that there are infinite particles or particles infinitely tiny inside a finite body. In order not to undermine

the structure of things in general and, in the case of compound formations, to avoid being compelled to fritter away existing things by compressing them into nothingness, we must accordingly give up the idea of infinite divisibility into smaller and smaller particles. Nor can we even pass in thought from the small to the smaller *ad infinitum* in the case of finite bodies, because the moment one says there are infinite particles or particles infinitely tiny in a body, it becomes impossible to conceive how this could be so, and furthermore how could such a body still be finite in size? For it is obvious that the infinite particles are of certain sizes, and, however tiny they are, the body would also be infinite in size.

Also, since a finite body has an end point that is distinguishable if not actually visible, it is impossible to conceive that the point next in order is not of the same sort, nor is it possible, by moving forward point by point in this manner, to proceed mentally to infinity. We should also observe that the perceptual minimum is not of the same nature as a partite body, nor is it in every respect dissimilar. It occupies a certain common ground with partite bodies, but it has no discrete parts. If by virtue of this resemblance, or common ground, we suppose that we can make divisions in it – one on this side, another on that – the eye necessarily encounters only another minimal point of equal extension. We see these points one after another; beginning with the first, and we see them not as internally partite or as partite bodies touching other partite bodies but rather, in their own idiosyncratic way, as measurements of magnitude, more points constituting a larger body, fewer points a smaller body.

By the same token it must be assumed that the minimal parts of the atom play an analogous role. It is obvious that they differ in size from the perceptual minimum, but they have the same relationship. We have, of course, indicated on the analogy of phenomena that the atom has size; only we scaled it far down. Also, in our logical theorizing about atoms that we do not see, we should regard their minimal, uncompounded parts as the ultimate limits of matter, which provide in themselves, as fundamental units, the measure of magnitude for atoms of all sizes, whether large or small. The common relationship that these minimal parts share with empirical minima suffices to bring the present discussion to a conclusion. In any case it is impossible that such particles were ever endowed with independent motion or that they coalesced into atoms.

3. Motion of Atoms. Furthermore, the atoms necessarily have equal velocities whenever they are propelled through empty space, where they meet with no resistance. Thus heavy atoms will not move any faster than small, light ones – at least when nothing collides with them – nor will small atoms move faster than large ones but will maintain a uniform rate of motion so long as they encounter no resistance. Upward or diagonal motion that is brought about by collisions is no faster, nor is the downward motion that is caused by their respective weights. So long as any of these motions obtains, the atom will maintain a velocity as fast as a

man can think, until it is deflected by something external or by its own mass recoiling from the force of an
impact. Furthermore, in its transit through space under
conditions where it meets with no bodies likely to
oppose it, it completes any determinate distance in an
inconceivably brief period of time; for the appearance of
relative slowness and speed is created by external resistance and nonresistance.

In addition, the claim will be made in the case of
compounds that one atom moves more rapidly than
another (when actually they all have the same velocity)
because the atoms in such collections move in one direction even during the smallest continuous period of
time that is perceptible. This claim will be made despite
the fact that atoms do not move in one direction during
time spans that are so brief as to be only mentally conceivable. On the contrary, they are in constant internal
collision [and by these collisions they retard the motion
of the whole collection] until such time as their path
becomes perceptible as a continuum. The inference
made regarding the subempirical level, viz., that time
spans that are mentally conceivable will also show a
continuous path, is not true in cases such as these, since
'true' means either that which is empirically observed
or that which is mentally apprehended.

Nor is it true in the case of these mentally conceivable
time spans that the moving object also completes the
same large number of trajectories as its component
atoms; this is inconceivable. Furthermore such an
object, on arriving as a unit at a perceived moment of

35

time from any given quarter of infinite space, will not have started from the spot from which we see it coming. The moving object will thus be the sensory counterpart of its internal collisions, even though we grant that up to the moment of perception its velocity is not subject to retardation because of such collisions. It will prove useful to keep this principle in mind also.

In addition, we should not predicate 'up' and 'down' of infinite space, as though there were an absolute standard of highest and lowest. Assuming, however, that it is possible to prolong to infinity a line overhead from wherever we may be standing or a line to infinity beneath a hypothetical point, we know that this segment of space will never appear to us to be simultaneously 'up' and 'down' with reference to the same assumed point, because this is inconceivable. Consequently it is possible to take the motion that we regard as infinite motion upward as a single entity, and the motion we regard as infinite motion downward as a single entity, even though in thousands of cases what travels from us into the spaces overhead arrives at the feet of beings above us and what travels downward from us reaches the heads of beings below us. Despite this fact, this is the case because we regard these motions, taken as wholes, as opposed each to the other *ad infinitum*.

VI. THE SOUL AND ITS NATURE

By referring to our sensations and feelings, which will provide the most reliable basis for our beliefs, we must next take into account the fact that the soul is a body composed of fine particles that are dispersed throughout the entire organism, and that it bears the closest resemblance to breath with a certain admixture of heat, being similar in some ways to the one and in some ways to the other. There is also a third component that shows an even greater difference in fineness of structure than the other two and is for this reason more adapted to the rest of the organism. This is all clearly evidenced by the functions and affections of the soul, by the ease of its movements and thought processes, and by the privations that cause our death.

In addition you must bear in mind that the soul plays the most important role in causing sensation but would never have achieved sensation unless it were somehow incorporated in the rest of the organism. The latter in turn, after providing the soul with this ground for sensation, has itself come to participate in the same function, thanks to the soul, but not in all the functions that the soul has. Hence when death releases the soul, the body does not have sensation, because it never possessed this capacity in and of itself but made it possible for another entity, generated at the same time as itself, to have sensation. This second entity, by actualizing its own potentiality through motion, at once achieved the function of sensation for itself and imparted it to the body also as a result of its proximity and congruence with the latter, as I said before.

Hence as long as the soul is present it will never cease to have sensation, even though some other part of the organism has been removed. On the contrary, if the soul persists at all it will have sensation, whatever particles of it are lost at the same time as its bodily casing is destroyed either in whole or in part. The rest of the organism, on the other hand, may continue to exist in whole or in part but will no longer have sensation once it has lost the mass of atoms, whatever its size, that constitutes the nature of the soul. Furthermore, on the dissolution of the entire organism the soul is scattered abroad and no longer has its usual functions, nor does it undergo motion, with the result that it does not have sensation either. It is impossible to think of it as sentient if it is not present in a composite whole and if it does not enjoy its usual movements at such times as its housing and environment are not the same as the present environment in which it carries out these movements.

In addition, we should note that in the ordinary usage of the term, 'incorporeal' is used of something that can be thought of as a thing in itself, and that it is impossible to think of the incorporeal as a thing in itself except in the case of empty space. Now, empty space can neither act upon nor be acted upon; it merely presents the opportunity for bodies to move through it. Hence those who maintain that the soul is incorporeal are talking nonsense, because it would not be able to act upon or be acted upon if it were of such a nature; but in actuality both these functions are clearly distinguishable in the case of the soul.

Now, if one refers all these observations about the soul to empirical standards of feeling and sensation, and recalls what was said at the beginning of this letter, he will see that this outline is sufficiently comprehensive for him to elaborate the details with precision from what is said here.

VII. PROPERTIES AND ACCIDENTS (L9)

Next, as regards the characteristics of shape, color, size, weight, and all the other qualities that are predicated of body as so-called 'concomitants' or properties of all bodies in general or of bodies that can be seen and are known to us as a result of perceiving these qualities: We should not think of these as self-existent essences (for this is inconceivable) or as completely nonexistent or as immaterial entities having a different existence from body and supervening upon it or as detachable parts of body. On the contrary, we should think of a body in its wholeness as having its own lasting existence from all these – not as though it were an assemblage of properties that had been brought together (as when a larger aggregate is put together from the component parts themselves, such as the primary particles or other quantities smaller than a given whole) but simply, as I said, as having its own lasting existence from all these. All these properties, furthermore, can be observed in their own right and distinguished, as long as the object as a whole accompanies such perception and is in no way detached but takes on the predicate 'body' from our thinking of its qualities as a whole.

In addition, bodies frequently have accidental

characteristics which are not permanent concomitants and which we should not regard as coming under the head of entities that are invisible, imperceptible, or non-material. Consequently when we use the term 'accident' in its ordinary sense, we are making it obvious that these contingencies have neither the nature of the whole object that we apprehend in its entirety and call 'body' nor the nature of those permanent properties in whose absence body is inconceivable. Assuming that the object as a whole is present, each of these contingencies might be called an accident as a result of various acts of perception, but only when they are each observed to occur, since accidents are not permanent concomitants. Also, we should not deny existence to these clear and distinct phenomena on the ground that they do not have the nature of the whole object of which they are accidents or the nature of permanent properties. Nor, on the other hand, should we regard them as things in themselves, because this is unthinkable in the case of both accidents and permanent properties. On the contrary, we should think of them all as accidents associated with bodies, as our senses indicate – not as permanent properties, not as entities having natural status as things in themselves, but as what perception itself shows their peculiar nature to be.

We must take great pains to note in addition that we should not investigate the nature of time as we do all the other properties and accidents of an object that we inquire into, i.e., by reference to concepts we have in our minds. On the contrary, we should consider those clear and distinct impressions in the light of which we speak of 'a long time' or 'a short time' and apply those impressions to time as we do in analogous cases. Nor should we substitute other expressions that are supposedly better, but use the already existing ones. Nor should we predicate some other entity of time, as some do, on the assumption that it has the same essence as this unique quality. Rather we should give our attention exclusively to what we associate this unique quality with and what we measure it by. Actually it requires no proof, simply reflection, to see, first, that we connect time with day and night or portions of these, and also with states of emotion or freedom from emotion, and with states of motion and rest; and, second, that we regard it as a unique type of accident associated with all these phenomena and accordingly give it the name 'time.'

VIII. OTHER WORLDS

In addition to the foregoing, we should consider that other worlds – i.e., every finite aggregate that bears a strong resemblance to the phenomena we see – have been generated from the infinite; that all these systems, whether large or small, disengaged themselves from separate condensations of matter; and that they are all broken down again into their components – some more rapidly, others more slowly, some being acted upon by factors of one sort, others by factors of another sort. Also we should consider that these worlds do not necessarily have a single form [or, on the other hand, every possible form; furthermore, that in all these worlds there are animals, plants, and other things such as we see in our own world]. For nobody can demonstrate that one such world might or might not have contained the kind of seminal particles of which animals, plants, and everything else we see are composed, but that in another such world this would have been an impossibility.

IX. GROWTH OF LANGUAGE AND CULTURE

Also, we must assume that at first actual conditions taught and compelled mankind to do many things of various sorts, and that later on reasoning perfected nature's instructions and made additional discoveries, more rapidly in some cases than in others and with greater progress in some periods than in others. Thus the names of things were not originally created by convention. On the contrary, the various ethnic groups of mankind, on experiencing their own peculiar emotions and sensory impressions, uttered sounds conforming to these various emotions and impressions, each in its own way, corresponding to the geographical differences of the groups. But later on, characteristic terms were assigned by common agreement in the various ethnic groups in order to make their intentions mutually more intelligible and to convey them more concisely. Also, people who knew them brought in certain things never seen before and suggested certain words for them. Sometimes these persons were forced to invent natural sounds for the objects; at other times they chose the sounds by a rational process in conformance with ordinary conventions, thereby clarifying their meaning.

X. THE HEAVENLY BODIES

Furthermore, we should not regard the courses and revolutions of the heavenly bodies – their eclipses, risings and settings, and the like – as the operations of some deity who dutifully performs these functions, who decrees or did decree them, and who simultaneously enjoys absolute blessedness as well as immortality. (For management of business affairs, worries, feelings of anger, and goodwill do not harmonize with the state of blessedness but are found where there is lack of strength and where we fear and have need of those around us.) Nor, on the other hand, should one imagine that these bodies, which are actually aggregations of fiery matter, enjoy divine blessedness themselves and take on these motions by an act of will. On the contrary, we must preserve the full dignity of the divine in all expressions we use in connection with ideas such as these, in order that notions contradictory to the divine majesty may not arise from this source; otherwise this very contradictoriness will produce the gravest spiritual disturbances. Hence we should hold the opinion that this necessary cyclical movement of the heavenly bodies came about through the original enclosure of these collections of matter at the genesis of the world.

In addition, we must consider that it is the task of natural science to determine with precision the causes of the most important phenomena and that our happiness is bound up with causal knowledge of the heavenly bodies, i.e., with the understanding of the nature of celestial phenomena, and everything else that is germane to scientific knowledge relating to human happiness. We should also realize that phenomena that have a variety of causes and can occur in more than one way do not belong here. On the contrary, anything that suggests uncertainty or confusion has absolutely no place in our conception of the deathless and blessed nature of the divine. This point can be rationally apprehended with complete certainty. On the other hand, everything that falls under the detailed investigation of the risings and settings of these bodies – their revolutions, eclipses, and kindred phenomena – makes no contribution to the happiness associated with causal knowledge. On the contrary, those who have observed such phenomena, but are ignorant of their nature and ultimate causes, stand in awe of them as much as if they had no knowledge of them; and their fear may well be greater if the wonderment occasioned by observation of such phenomena fails to find an explanation in a system of ultimate causes. Hence even if we find more than one cause for these revolutions, risings, settings, eclipses, and the like, as we did in our detailed treatise, we must not suppose that we have not acquired the scientific knowledge needed to contribute to our serenity and happiness. Hence we should investigate the causes of all celestial and nonperceptible phenomena by making a comparison of these with the various ways in which an analogous phenomenon takes place in our own experience. And we should hold a low opinion of those who fail to distinguish between phenomena having a single cause and, in the case of objects making a sensory impression on us from a distance, phenomena that have more than one cause; and a low opinion also of those who are ignorant of the conditions in which it is impossible to have an undisturbed mind. Accordingly if we suppose that it is possible for an event to take place in one particular way, under conditions where it is equally possible for us to feel unconcerned if we recognize that it may have more than one cause, we shall feel as undisturbed as if we knew that it occurs in one particular way.

XI. CONCLUSION

In addition to all these general considerations we must realize that the most important types of spiritual confusion consist (1) in men's believing that the heavenly bodies are themselves blessed and immortal and at the same time have wills, activities, and motives that are contrary to such properties (2) in their constantly anticipating or imagining some frightful everlasting fate, like those in the myths of hell, or dreading the loss of sensation at the time of death as though this were relevant to 'themselves', and (3) in undergoing all this suffering not as a result of rational judgment but because of some irrational drive (and by not setting limits to mental suffering, they consequently experience turmoil equal to or even more intense than they would if they rationally entertained such beliefs). But mental serenity means achieving release from all such fears and keeping the most important general principles constantly in mind.

Thus we should give our attention to our immediate feelings and sensations, in both their general and their particular aspects, according to the circumstances, and to our existing clear and distinct perceptions, in conformance with each of the criteria of judgment. If we attend to these we shall correctly discern the causes that gave rise to confusion and fear, and by investigating the causes of celestial phenomena and all the other occurrences that are constantly taking place we shall liberate ourselves from everything that drives other men to the extremes of fear.

These are the main topics of my system as a whole, Herodotus, which I have epitomized for you in such a way that the present account can be comprehended with precision. In my opinion, even if a person did not go on to study all the scientific details, he would still enjoy an incomparable advantage over others, because he would make clear to himself many of the points that are investigated in detail in my general treatise, and these, once deposited in the memory, will be of constant assistance to him. These principles are of such a nature that those who are already studying the system in considerable or complete detail can do most of their research into the structure of the whole by analysis along these lines. On the other hand, some of those who are not fully matured Epicureans can promote their spiritual tranquility by making a rapid survey of the essentials through this voiceless method.

Letter to Pythocles

Cleon brought me a letter from you in which you continue to show affectionate regard for me commensurate with my own feelings toward you and in which you rather convincingly attempt to recall the lines of reasoning that tend to promote the happy life. You ask me to send you a sketch or concise account of celestial phenomena for easy review. You say that what I have written elsewhere on the subject is hard to remember, even though you claim that my books are constantly in your hands. I greeted your request with pleasure and feel obliged to comply with it because of my fond hopes for you. Since I have finished all my other writing I shall therefore carry out your wishes, with the expectation that this account will be serviceable to many others also, especially those who have recently come into contact with genuine natural science as well as people who are rather deeply involved in everyday business affairs. Consider it well, then, and go through it systematically, bearing the various points in mind together with my other remarks in the shorter epitome that I sent to Herodotus.

I. PROCEDURE

First of all, then, we must assume that no other end is served by the study of celestial phenomena, whether considered by themselves or in some larger context, than mental composure and a sturdy self-reliance, just as in the case of the other disciplines.

We must not force an impossible explanation on these phenomena or make our treatment similar in all respects to an ethical discourse or to an explication of the problems of noncelestial physics – as seen, for example, in the statements 'The universe consists of bodies and an intangible substance' or 'Atoms are indivisible' and in all other such cases where there is but a single explanation that is consistent with phenomena. This is not the case with the heavenly bodies. Their origins have more than one cause, and there is more than one set of predications relating to their nature that is compatible with our sensory experience. We should not carry on the study of nature by means of meaningless axioms and scientific decrees but should allow phenomena to elicit their own explanations; for we have no use now for personal prejudice and meaningless guesswork if we are to live the unperturbed life. In the case of occurrences which have more than one explanation that is consistent with the phenomena, nothing need shake our composure if we are willing to concede, as we must, that theories about them are only probable. But if a person takes one explanation and throws out another that is equally compatible with the phenomenon, it is obvious that he is departing completely from scientific procedure and has slipped into religious superstition. From terrestrial phenomena it is possible to derive certain indications of what takes place in the heavenly bodies. It can be observed how the former occur but not how celestial phenomena occur, because it is possible for the latter to happen from a variety of causes. However, we must give heed to the sensory impression in each case, and in our judgments connected with it we must determine those cases where multiple causation is not contradicted by terrestrial phenomena.

II. WORLDS

A world is a circumscribed section of the heavens and includes a sun, moon, stars, an earth, and all that occurs in the heavens; at its dissolution everything in it will be thrown into disorder. It is a segment of infinite space and terminates in a periphery that is either rarefied or dense, either in circular motion or in a state of rest, either spherical or triangular or of any other shape. All these possibilities exist, inasmuch as they are not contradicted by any phenomenon in our own world where it is impossible to lay hold of a terminal point.

Furthermore, we can readily grasp the fact that such worlds are infinite in number and that any such world may be generated within a world or in the cosmic interspaces (i.e., the spaces between worlds) in a region containing a good deal of empty space but not in a pure vacuum of great size, as some persons claim. The birth of a world occurs after the necessary atoms have streamed in from one or more worlds or interspaces, gradually form organized aggregates, and effect the transfer of matter to various areas of the system as chance dictates, feeding in the appropriate materials until the world is completed. It then remains in equilibrium as long as the foundations that have been laid down are capable of receiving additional matter. Thus the formation of a world requires more than merely a congregating of atoms and a vortex in a vacuum supposedly generated by Necessity. Nor can a world keep on growing until it collides with another world, as one of the so-called cosmologists claims, because this runs counter to our experience.

III. THE HEAVENLY BODIES

1. Their Creation, Size, Movements, etc. The sun, moon, and other heavenly bodies were not generated separately and incorporated later into the world, but were formed at once and augmented by the conjunctions of swirling masses composed of tiny particles having the nature of air or fire or both; for this is what the senses suggest. The size of the sun, moon, and other heavenly bodies is from our point of view just what it appears to be. From an absolute point of view it is either somewhat greater than what we see or somewhat smaller or exactly the same, because this is the way that fiery objects on earth appear to the senses when viewed from a distance. Any objection to this part of the argument will easily be resolved if we attend to our clear and distinct perceptions, as I point out in my work *On Nature*.

The risings and settings of the sun, the moon, and the other heavenly bodies may come about from the lighting up and quenching of their fires, if the conditions at the place of their rising or setting are such as to bring about the aforementioned effects; for nothing in our sensory experience runs counter to this hypothesis. Or the said effects may be caused by the emergence of these bodies from a point above the earth and again by the earth's position in front of them; for nothing in our sensory experience is against this.

It is not impossible that the movements of these bodies may occur because of the rotation of the heavens as a whole, or the latter may be stationary and the heavenly bodies may rotate because of the necessary eastward motion that was generated originally at the birth of the world.

It is possible that the tropics, or turning points of the sun and moon, are brought about by the slanting of the sky, which is forced into this position by the seasons; or, equally possible, by transverse air currents; or because the right sort of fuel is always ignited in due order as the previous supply leaves off burning; or because this kind of rotary motion was originally forced upon these bodies, with the result that they move in a kind of spiral.

Now, none of these theories or theories related to these are incompatible with our clear and distinct perceptions of things, provided we hold to the possible in these matters and are able to refer each theory to some phenomenal counterpart and not stand in awe of the slavish fabrications of the astronomers.

2. The Moon. The waning and waxing of the moon may take place because of this body's rotation, or, equally well, because of the structure of the atmosphere, or again because some other body places itself in front of the moon. In fact, the phases of the moon may occur in any of the ways in which events in our own experience prompt us to give an account of this lunar phenomenon, provided we do not become overly fond of the 'one cause' principle and irresponsibly reject other explanations without first considering what can and what cannot be observed, and consequently end up desiring to observe the impossible.

Again, it is possible that the moon may have her own light and also possible that she has it from the sun, because in our own experience we observe many objects that have their own light and many that get light from other sources. No celestial phenomenon stands in the way of these hypotheses, if we always keep in mind the principle of multiple causation and consider as a group the causal hypotheses that are relevant to the events, and do not concentrate on the irrelevant and rashly exaggerate it or lean in one way or another to the 'one cause' method.

The apparent face in the moon may be caused by the

variation of its physical features or by some object in front of the moon or by any one of a number of observable factors that harmonize with phenomena on earth. Thus one should never neglect this method of investigation in the case of the heavenly bodies, because if a person fights the clear evidence of his senses he will never be able to share in genuine tranquility.

3. Eclipses, Periods, etc. An eclipse of the sun or moon may occur because of the dying out of its fires, a thing we see occurring on earth also; or from other bodies passing in front of them, such as the earth or some invisible object or something else of this sort. We must thus consider as a group explanations that belong together and recognize that the simultaneous conjunction of certain causes is not an impossibility.

Again, the regularity of the celestial periods is comparable to the way in which certain occurrences take place in our own experience. The divine nature, once more, should never be brought into these events. Let us exempt it from such responsibilities and keep it in the full state of blessedness. If we fail to do this, our whole causal theory regarding celestial phenomena will be meaningless, as it has already become for those who have not availed themselves of the method of possibility. These persons have resorted to the meaningless practice of thinking that things happen only in one way and of rejecting all the other methods that accord with the principle of the possible. They turn to the irrational and are unable to examine the terrestrial phenomena that we must accept as the analogues of celestial occurrences.

The varying length of night and day may be caused by the fact that the sun's movements over the earth are alternately fast and slow because it crosses areas of varying length or passes over certain areas more rapidly than others. There are analogous cases in our own experience, and in speaking of the heavenly bodies our theories must harmonize with such cases. Those who hold to one cause, however, resist such evidence and have failed to observe whether it is possible for human beings to use the empirical method.

IV. METEOROLOGY

Weather Signs, Clouds, Rain, Lightning, etc.

1. Weather signs may occur through a conjunction of events (as in the case of animals seen by all of us) and also from alterations and changes in the atmosphere. Neither of these runs counter to experience, but it is impossible to determine which particular cause operates under given conditions.

2. Clouds may be brought together and generated by the thickening of the atmosphere under wind pressure, by the twining together of the interlocking atoms needed to bring about this effect, or by the collecting of streams of moisture from the earth and its waters; in addition, there are several other ways in which such formations may quite possibly occur. Once clouds are formed, rain water may be produced from them if certain areas are compressed or if they undergo certain

other changes. Another cause of rain is the downflow of winds moving through the atmosphere out of the right quarter. Heavier precipitation is caused by the atomic aggregations needed for such downpours.

3. It is possible that thunder may be caused by the rolling around of the wind in the hollows of the clouds (analogously to our own storage jars); by the booming of wind-inflated fire inside the clouds; by the rupturing and tearing apart of clouds; or by the rubbing together and fracturing of clouds after they have taken on an icelike solidity. Empirical considerations call upon us to apply the principle of multiple causation to this department of meteorology as we do in general.

4. Lightning is likewise caused in several ways: (1) Because of the rubbing together and colliding of clouds, the fire-producing configuration of atoms escapes and generates lightning, and the atomic bodies that produced this flash are hurled out of the clouds by winds; or the cause may be a squeezing-out process that takes place when the clouds are compressed either by each other or by winds. (2) The light that is disseminated by the heavenly bodies may be enclosed in the clouds, then become concentrated by the motion of clouds and winds, and fall out through the clouds; or light composed of extremely fine particles may filter through the clouds, and in this way the clouds may be ignited by the fire and thunder be produced by the fire's motion. (3) Wind may be ignited by its intensity of motion and violent swirling about; or clouds may be shattered by winds, and the fire-producing atoms may fall out,

causing the phenomenon of lightning. In addition, it will be easy to discover several other ways if we hold consistently to the evidence of the senses and are able to observe there what resembles the celestial events.

In cloud conditions such as these, lightning precedes thunder (1) because the atomic configuration that causes the lightning is thrust out at the same time as the wind rushes in, and subsequently the swirling wind produces the boom of thunder; or (2) because they are both ejected simultaneously, but lightning moves toward us at a greater velocity, with the thunder following after, analogously to certain objects that are seen at a distance and make differing sensory impacts.

5. Thunderbolts may possibly occur (1) because of dense accumulations of winds that swirl about and ignite in a powerful flame, a portion of which is ripped loose and descends violently to the ground below (the breaking loose of the bolt occurs because the masses of cloud become increasingly close packed, owing to compression); or (2) because of the actual ejection of the swirling fire (comparable to the way thunder is produced), when the flame becomes too massive and too violently inflated with wind; it then ruptures the cloud, since it is unable to go back to the adjoining areas because of the steady compression of the cloud masses one against the other. And it is possible that thunderbolts may be caused in still other ways. Only let there be an end to mythologizing! And there will be if we rightly follow the evidence of the senses in gleaning hints about things unseen.

6. Cyclones may be caused (1) by the descent of a

cloud in the form of a column to the earth below, the cloud being thrust downward by compacted wind and driven by massive gusts, while at the same time the wind outside it pushes it sideways; (2) by the formation of the wind into a spiral, air being forced down upon it from above; or (3) when a strong current of wind is generated and is unable to flow through the cloud mass sideways because of the compression of the atmosphere around it. When the cyclonic winds reach down as far as the earth, whirlwinds of every sort are generated corresponding to the various wind motions, whereas over the sea waterspouts result.

7. Earthquakes may be caused (1) by the trapping of wind in the earth, the displacing of the ground in small masses, and the adjacent motion, all of which produces a quaking of the earth. The latter either takes in this wind from the outside and encloses it, or else chunks of ground fall into cavernous depressions in the earth and churn up the air trapped there. In addition, (2) it is possible for earthquakes to be produced by the actual diffusion of the motion caused by the caving in of masses of earth and the countermotion that occurs when the former meets with thick concentrations of earth. There are also many other ways in which these movements of the earth may occur.

*

8. Hail is caused (1) by a process of heavy freezing when certain wind particles are grouped together from all

around and then broken up into pellets; or (2) by a more moderate freezing of water particles accompanied by a breaking-up process – in other words, the simultaneous compression and splitting up of the hailstones, with the effect that both the parts and the wholes solidify as they freeze. The roundness of the stones may quite possibly be caused by the sharp points melting away all around or because at the time of their formation (so the claim goes) certain water particles or wind particles are evenly compounded in a circle, part by part.

9. Snow may be caused (1) by fine rain precipitating from the clouds through pores of suitable size due to strong wind pressure on the right sort of clouds; this rain then assumes a frozen state in transit due to certain conditions of intense cold in the clouds at lower levels. Due to freezing in clouds which have a uniform porosity, precipitation of this sort might be produced (2) by rain clouds that lie side by side and press against each other, just as they produce hail by causing compression, a very frequent atmospheric occurrence. Due to the friction of clouds that have assumed a frozen state, this snow formation (3) may be whirled off. And there are still other ways in which it is possible for snow to be produced.

10. Dew is produced (1) by the coming together of those atmospheric particles that are productive of this kind of moisture and (2) by the evaporation of particles from damp spots or places containing water, in which dew is generally produced. These water-bearing

particles then come together, produce moisture, and again precipitate to the earth below, a phenomenon we see occurring in many cases in our own experience. In addition, frost is produced when drops of dew are altered in such a way as to assume a kind of frozen state due to the circumstance that the atmosphere is cold.

11. Ice is produced (1) by the extrusion of particles of round formation from water and the compression of the uneven and acute-angled particles existent in the water; (2) by the assimilation from outside of particles of the latter sort, which on being forced together cause freezing in the water by pressing out a certain number of round particles.

12. The rainbow is produced (1) by sunlight shining on an atmosphere full of water particles; or (2) by a special combination of light and air that often causes the special characteristics of these colors, either collectively or severally; because it reflects light, the adjacent areas of the atmosphere will often take on the coloring we see, due to the shining of the light on its various parts. The well-known phenomenon of the rainbow's circularity is caused by the fact that the eye sees it at an equal distance from all its points or (2) because the atoms in the air or those in the clouds that are received from sunlight have become compressed in this way and the combination of the two stretches earthward in a kind of circle.

13. A halo around the moon is produced (1) when air advances from every quarter toward the moon; or (2) when the atmosphere holds back effluvia discharged by

the moon, uniformly and in such a way as to spread them around in a circle in this cloudlike formation, with no inequalities whatsoever; or (3) when it holds back the atmosphere around the moon symmetrically at every point, so as to spread it thickly in a circle. This occurs in various parts of the sky either because some external current forces the air around or because heat stops up the atmospheric channels in a way necessary to produce this effect.

V. MISCELLANEOUS
CELESTIAL PHENOMENA

Comets, Fixed Stars, Planets, etc.

1. Comets occur (1) when fire accumulates in certain areas of the upper air during certain periods, after the occurrence of a certain atomic formation; (2) because the heavens overhead have a particular motion at certain times, with the result that stars of this sort become visible; (3) because they start to move independently at certain times because of special circumstances and come into areas of the heavens over us and thus become visible. The disappearance of these bodies is brought about by causes opposite to the above.

2. Certain stars 'turn on the very spot'. This comes about (1) not merely because this part of the world is fixed and the rest of the sky revolves around it (as some maintain) but also because a vortex of air encircles it, which is an impediment to their ranging about as the

other stars do; or (2) because they do not have the necessary supply of fuel except in this region of the sky where we see that they are fixed. There are also a number of other ways in which it is possible for this phenomenon to occur, provided we are able to make deductions that are consistent with the evidence of the senses.

3. The fact that certain of the stars are planets, or 'wanderers' (if such is actually the case), whereas certain others do not have these erratic movements, may possibly be explained as follows: (1) Necessity from the very beginning compelled some of them, as they moved in their circular paths, to rotate in the same regular orbits and forced others at the same time to follow courses that have certain irregularities. (2) It is also possible that in some of the regions where they move there are level stretches of atmosphere that successively thrust them forward in the same direction by providing a uniform supply of fuel, as well as other stretches that are uneven, with the result that the deviations in orbit that we observe are brought about. Application of the 'one cause' method to these events, when the phenomena call for multiple explanation, is a mad and improper practice of persons who have espoused the worthless science of astrology and who reduce causal theory to meaninglessness when they fail to release the deity from such duties.

4. The fact that certain stars are observed to lag behind others comes about (1) because they move in the same circular orbit but rotate more slowly than the

others, (2) because they move in the opposite direction but are held back by the revolution of the other stars, or (3) because all stars traverse the same circular path, but some rotate over a greater area, others over a lesser. To offer the simple 'one cause' explanation of such phenomena is appropriate for people who want to parade their superstitions before the mob.

5. So-called falling stars may be caused in part (1) by a collision of stars and the subsequent falling out of debris, which occurs whenever there is a discharge of wind, as we remarked in connection with lightning; (2) by an aggregation of atoms that produce fire (assuming that there has been a meeting of cognate bodies to this end) and by their fall in the direction of the original impetus imparted to them by their coming together; (3) by a concourse of winds in dense, mistlike concentrations; this mass then ignites because of compression, bursts out of the surrounding matter, and falls toward whatever region its impetus carries it. And there are still other ways in which this phenomenon may occur, ways that have nothing to do with myth.

6. The weather signs provided by certain animals come about through a conjunction of events, since animals do not bring any influence to bear on winter's coming to an end, nor does some divine being sit and watch them coming out of hibernation and then bring these portents to pass! Not even an insignificant creature would be guilty of such stupidity (though trifles give more pleasure, they say), not to mention a being that has attained to perfect happiness.

VI. CONCLUSION

If you remember these various points, Pythocles, you will keep clear of religious superstition for the most part and be able to comprehend related matters. Devote yourself particularly to the study of metaphysical origins, infinity, and kindred topics, as well as the criteria of truth, the feelings, and the purpose for which we reflect on all these matters. It is particularly the synoptic view of these topics as a group that will make it easy for you to study causation in detail. But those who have not fully committed themselves emotionally to these matters cannot properly view them as they are, nor have they grasped the purpose and the need for studying them.